THE POCKET GUIDE

Discover the Wonders of the Esmerald Isle: from Enchanting Landscapes to Fashinating Culture, Food, and

Age-Old Traditions.

By

KIMONS

© **Copyright KIMONS -2023 - All rights reserved.**

The content contained within this book may not be reproduced, duplicated, or transmitted without direct written permission from the author or the publisher. Under no circumstances will any blame or legal responsibility be held against the publisher, or author, for any damages, reparation, or monetary loss due to the information contained within this book, either directly or indirectly.

Legal Notice: This book is copyright protected. It is only for personal use. You cannot amend, distribute, sell, use, quote, or paraphrase any part of the content within this book without the consent of the author or publisher.

Disclaimer Notice: Please note the information contained within this document is for educational and entertainment purposes only. All effort has been executed to present accurate, up-to-date, reliable, and complete information. No warranties of any kind are declared or implied. Readers acknowledge that the author is not engaging in the rendering of legal, financial, medical, or professional advice.

The content within this book has been derived from various sources. Please consult a licensed professional before attempting any techniques outlined in this book. By reading this document, the reader agrees that under no circumstances is the author responsible for any losses, direct or indirect, that are incurred as a result of the use of the information contained within this document, including, but not limited to, errors, omissions, or inaccuracies.

TABLE OF CONTENT

CHAPTER 1: Introduction to Ireland 7

   1.1 Geography 7

   1.2 Climate 8

   1.3 Demographics 11

   1.4 Politics 14

CHAPTER 2: Main Destinations 17

   2.1 Dublin 17

      2.1.1 St. Patrick's Cathedral 22

      2.1.2 The Guinness Storehouse 24

      2.1.3 The National Museum of Ireland 26

   2.2 Galway 28

   2.3 The Giant's Causeway and Antrim Coast 31

   2.4 Cork and the Ring of Kerry 36

   2.5 The Cliffs of Moher 38

   2.6 Glendalough Valley 41

   2.7 Donegal and the Wild Atlantic Way 43

   2.8 Killarney National Park 44

   2.9 The City of Kilkenny 46

   2.10 Connemara and the Aran Islands 47

      2.10.1 Kylemore Castle 50

CHAPTER 3: Irish Gastronomy 53

   3.1 Introduction to Irish Cuisine 53

   3.2 Irish Stew 54

3.3 Colcannon 57

3.4 Oysters 60

3.5 Guinness 62

3.6 Where to Find the Best Local Cuisine 65

CHAPTER 4: Local history.. 67

4.1 The Celts and Irish Culture 67

4.2 The Viking Invasion 69

4.3 The Norman Era and the Kingdom of Ireland 71

4.4 English Domination and the Great Famine 73

4.5 The Fight for Independence and Modern Ireland........... 75

CHAPTER 5: Culture and Traditions... 79

5.1 Holidays such as Saint Patrick's Day................................ 79

5.2 Legends of the Leprechaun.. 81

5.3 Folk Music 83

5.4 Gaelic Language 85

5.5 Literature 87

5.6 Irish Dance 90

CHAPTER 6: **Travel Advice.. 93**

6.1 The Best Time to Visit Ireland 93

6.2 Transportation... 95

6.3 What to Pack.. 97

6.4 Local Norms and Customs to Respect........................... 100

CHAPTER 7: Useful Information on Credit Cards and Currency
...104

7.1 Accepted Credit Cards... 104

7.2 Cash Withdrawals 106

7.3 Currency Exchange 108

7.4 Currency Management 110

7.5 Useful Information on Credit Cards and Money 111

Conclusion... 113

Recommended itineraries (bonus).. 118

CHAPTER 1: Introduction to Ireland

1.1 Geography

Immerse yourself with me in the heart of Europe, where the Atlantic Ocean meets the mainland, giving life to emerald green landscapes, rolling hills, and jagged coasts. Here arises Ireland, a jewel nestled in the northwest of the continent, an island of mystery, magic, and indescribable natural beauty. Ireland is not a simple geographical unit, but rather a mosaic of territories and stories. The island is divided in two: the Republic of Ireland, which occupies most of the island, and Northern Ireland, the northeastern part of the island that remains firmly tied to the United Kingdom. This division, however, is more political than geographical, and for the traveler crossing the island, the differences are subtle and almost imperceptible.

The Emerald Isle, as it is affectionately known,

is a collage of diverse and fascinating landscapes. The interior lands are studded with not-too-high mountains, with the Wicklow mountains standing as sentinels south of Dublin. These elevations gradually empty into vast green plains, dense with grazing sheep and dotted with picturesque villages.

Ireland is a land of rivers and lakes. The Shannon River, the longest in the country, winds through the heart of Ireland, creating a series of beautiful lakes along its course. The plains then transform into spectacular coastal cliffs, where the land meets the Atlantic in a dramatic contrast of rock and water.

Throughout your travels through Ireland, you will find terrains that speak of ancient legends and stories, each with its particular beauty and charm. This land promises adventures and discoveries, stories to tell, and memories to keep.

1.2 Climate

A journey through Ireland wouldn't be complete without experiencing its climate, a fundamental element that contributes to defining the uniqueness of the Emerald Isle. Describing the Irish climate is not a simple task. It's never too hot, nor too cold. It's never too dry, nor too humid. The Irish climate, like its inhabitants, is a fascinating example of balance and temperance.

Ireland, in its isolated splendor, is kissed by a temperate oceanic climate that makes it an ideal destination for those who prefer mild summers and gentle winters. Here, extreme temperatures are rare, replaced by a pleasant average temperature that rarely rises above 20 degrees in summer or falls below zero in winter.

The sea surrounding Ireland serves as a thermal stabilizer, ensuring that summer temperatures are cooler and winter temperatures milder than on the continent. This makes Ireland an ideal destination for those who want to escape the oppressive summer heat or the icy winter cold of other parts of Europe.

However, Ireland is also a land of nuances and

variations. The geographical location of the island places it directly in the path of Atlantic depressions, which bring with them rainfall throughout the year. It's not uncommon for a sunny sky to quickly turn into a downpour, only to shine brightly shortly after.

If there's one element that consistently accompanies the traveler in Ireland, it's rain. However, it's not monsoon-like rain. Rather, it's a light and thin rain, sometimes barely more than a mist, that can lend a veil of mystery and charm to the landscape. It's this constant rain that keeps Ireland so incredibly green, earning it the nickname of the Emerald Isle.

But don't be discouraged by the rain. The Irish rain is part of the travel experience, and there's a certain charm in taking refuge in a cozy pub when a shower starts to fall, or in walking along a deserted beach with only the sound of rain and waves as a backdrop.

In the coastal regions, fog can envelop the landscape, adding an almost mystical atmosphere to the cliffs and stacks. And in the winter months, the mountains inland can even be blanketed with snow, transforming the landscape into an almost fairy-tale scene.

Ultimately, the Irish climate is as changeable as it is fascinating. It creates shades of light and color that change rapidly, and offers a steady rhythm that beats the time of life on the island. Whether you're wrapped in a coat under a gray sky, or strolling in short sleeves under a radiant sun, the Irish climate will be an unforgettable part of your trip, adding an extra touch of character to an already charming island.

1.3 Demographics

Discovering Ireland doesn't just mean exploring its fascinating geography or understanding its changing climate, but also familiarizing yourself with the people who populate it. Ireland is a country of around 5 million inhabitants, a figure that might seem modest compared to other European nations, but it hides a vibrant mosaic of people, cultures, and stories.

One of the most impressive features of Ireland

is its population density. Despite Ireland being the third largest island in Europe, its population is relatively sparse, which means there are vast spaces of untouched nature to explore. This doesn't mean that Ireland lacks vibrant urban centers: Dublin, the capital, houses over a million inhabitants and buzzes with activity, its streets crowded with shops, restaurants, pubs, and museums.

Other significant cities include Cork, the second largest city and a major cultural hub; Galway, known for its lively pedestrian streets and vibrant arts scene; and Limerick, famous for its rich historical heritage. However, a significant portion of the Irish population lives in small towns or in rural areas, where farming remains a key aspect of daily life.

Linguistically, Ireland is a bilingual country. English is the dominant language and is spoken by everyone, but Irish (or Gaelic) is still alive and well, especially in the Gaeltacht areas, where Irish is the primary language. Even though only a small percentage of the population speaks Irish daily, the language is an essential part of Ireland's cultural heritage and is taught in schools throughout the country.

In terms of religion, Ireland is historically a strongly Catholic country. Although Irish society has become more secular in recent decades, most Irish people still identify as Catholic. However, tolerance and welcoming are key values in Irish society, and people of all faiths and none are welcomed.

Ireland is also a young country. With an average age of just over 36 years, the Irish population is one of the youngest in Europe. This can be seen in the vibrant youth districts of the cities, in world-class universities like Trinity College in Dublin, and in the lively arts and music scene of the country.

Getting to know Ireland means getting to know its people. From the crowded streets of Dublin to the quiet country roads, from the lively music scene to the quiet country churches, Ireland is a country of contrasts, a place where traditions of the past blend with aspirations for the future. And it's the people who live on this beautiful island that bring these contrasts to life, forming the unique and fascinating mosaic that is today's Ireland.

1.4 Politics

Ireland is a country that can boast a rich and turbulent political history, which has shaped its present and continues to influence its future. Understanding the Irish political landscape is crucial to understanding the country and its people, and to fully immersing oneself in the travel experience.

The Republic of Ireland is a parliamentary democracy. The head of state is the President, a largely ceremonial figure elected by the people for a term of seven years. The real political power, however, lies with the Taoiseach, the Prime Minister, who is the head of government. The Taoiseach is appointed by the Dáil Éireann, the lower house of parliament, which is elected by the Irish people.

The main Irish political parties are Fianna Fáil and Fine Gael, both center-right, followed by the Labour Party and Sinn Féin, a left-wing nationalist party. These parties represent a wide range of political opinions, from social issues to economic matters, and their policies and public support can vary considerably from one election to another.

One of the central themes of Irish politics in recent decades has been the relationship between the Republic of Ireland and Northern Ireland, which is part of the United Kingdom. This relationship has been defined by the complex peace process known as the Good Friday Agreement of 1998, which ended decades of violent conflict. Although the peace process has brought great stability, issues concerning Northern Ireland remain at the heart of Irish political debate.

Another significant issue in the Irish political landscape is European integration. Ireland has been a member of the European Union since 1973 and, over the years, has greatly benefited from European funds and access to the single market. Despite some controversies, such as the initial rejection of the Lisbon Treaty in 2008, Ireland generally remains strongly pro-European.

Politics in Ireland is a fascinating mosaic of ideas, people, and stories. Whether it's the lively election campaigns, the historic party rivalries, or the big national and European issues, politics is a vital aspect of Irish life. And as visitors, knowing this dimension of the country can only enrich our understanding and appreciation of Ireland.

CHAPTER 2: Main Destinations

2.1 Dublin

Immersing yourself in the pulsating energy of Dublin, Ireland's capital, is like leafing through the pages of an enchanting novel, where every chapter unveils new characters, stories, and settings. This vibrant city, situated on the eastern coast of the island, combines a rich historical heritage with a contemporary and lively atmosphere, creating a mosaic of experiences that draw visitors from around the world.

The heart of Dublin is undoubtedly Trinity College, the prestigious university that boasts former students such as Oscar Wilde and Samuel Beckett. Strolling through its historic square is like taking a step back in time, but it is the Trinity College Library that holds the real gem: the Book of Kells, a decorated manuscript dating back to the 9th century and one of the oldest in the world.

Not far away is the Guinness Storehouse, a

must-have experience for anyone visiting the city. Here, you can discover the history behind the famous Irish dark beer, follow the production process, and finally enjoy a pint in the Gravity Bar, with a panoramic view over all of Dublin. It is an experience that delights all the senses, filling the eyes with sights, the nose with the smell of malt, and the palate with the unmistakable taste of Guinness.

A trip to Dublin would not be complete without a visit to the vibrant Temple Bar district. During the day, its cobbled streets are an explosion of color, with craft shops, independent coffee shops, and outdoor markets. At night, Temple Bar transforms into the throbbing heart of Dublin's nightlife, with its numerous pubs filling the air with traditional Irish music.

Another landmark in Dublin is Dublin Castle, a historic building that has played a central role in Irish history since 1204. Now, it is a tourist site that hosts museums, art exhibitions, and the magnificent St. Patrick's Hall, the official ceremonial hall of the President of Ireland.

Finally, one cannot miss visiting St. Patrick's Cathedral, the largest cathedral in Ireland. Built in honor of Ireland's patron saint, St. Patrick's Cathedral is a masterpiece of Gothic architecture, with an interior as impressive as its external façade.

But Dublin is much more than these landmarks. It's a city that you discover by walking along its crowded streets, entering a small pub, talking to the locals, savoring a meal in one of its many gourmet restaurants, or listening to a street musician on Grafton Street. Every corner of Dublin has a story to tell, and all who visit this city end up becoming part of that story.

After exploring the historical heart of Dublin, it's time to dive into its vibrant cultural and social scene. The city is famous for its cozy pubs, many of which offer live sessions of traditional Irish music. Temple Bar is one of the most famous, but you'll find welcoming pubs in every corner of the city, each with its unique atmosphere. Be sure to taste a pint of Guinness, the famous Irish stout that is almost synonymous with Dublin itself.

Dublin is also a city of literature. It has been the birthplace of numerous famous writers, including James Joyce, Oscar Wilde, and Samuel Beckett, and has an entire area, called "Dublin's Literary Quarter", dedicated to its rich literary heritage. You can visit James Joyce's house, stroll through St. Stephen's Green imagining yourself in an Oscar Wilde novel, or participate in one of the many literary events that regularly take place in the city.

There is no shortage of opportunities for art enthusiasts in Dublin. The Dublin City Gallery The Hugh Lane hosts a wonderful collection of modern and contemporary art, while the National Gallery of Ireland boasts works by artists such as Rembrandt, Monet, and Picasso. If you're an art enthusiast, be sure to also visit the Museum of Contemporary Art (MOCA) and the Royal Hibernian Academy.

If you prefer outdoor activities, Dublin will not disappoint. Phoenix Park, one of the largest city parks in Europe, is a perfect place to take a walk, have a picnic, ride a bike, or simply relax. It is also home to the Dublin Zoo, Ashtown Castle, and the official residence of the President of Ireland.

Dublin is a city of contrasts, where the old coexists with the new, and the traditional mixes with the cosmopolitan. You can spend a morning exploring ancient manuscripts at the Chester Beatty Library, an afternoon shopping along Grafton Street or in the modern Docklands district, and an evening enjoying a comedy at one of the city's theaters or dining in one of its Michelin-starred restaurants.

But perhaps the most special thing about Dublin are its inhabitants. Dubliners are famous for their warm welcome and their sense of humor. They do not hesitate to chat, tell a story, or give directions to a lost tourist. They will make your trip to Dublin truly unforgettable.

So, if you're planning a trip to Ireland, make sure to include Dublin in your itinerary. Whether you're a lover of history, an art enthusiast, a connoisseur of food and drink, or simply a traveler in search of adventures, Dublin has something to offer you. And one thing is for sure: once you've experienced its unique atmosphere, you'll be eager to return.

2.1.1 St. Patrick's Cathedral

Located in the heart of Dublin, it is one of the architectural and spiritual jewels of Ireland. This imposing Gothic building, dedicated to the patron saint of Ireland, is a living testament to the island's rich history and religious heritage.

The majesty of the cathedral is evident in its imposing Gothic façade, characterized by sharp spires, intricate arches, and sculpted details that capture the attention of visitors at first glance. Once inside, the atmosphere is permeated with solemnity and spirituality, with its wide aisles, stained glass windows filtering divine light, and carefully decorated altars.

One of the most iconic features of the cathedral is its bell tower, which offers a breathtaking panoramic view of the city of Dublin. Climbing the narrow stairs of the tower is an exhilarating experience that rewards you with a spectacular panorama, allowing you to admire the enchanting Dublin skyline and its surroundings.

But St. Patrick's Cathedral is not just a place of worship, it is also a cultural center and a symbol of community life. It hosts concerts, cultural events, and art exhibitions that enliven its interior and create a vibrant and welcoming atmosphere.

For visitors who wish to immerse themselves in the history and spirituality of Ireland, a visit to St. Patrick's Cathedral is an absolute must. Be enchanted by the majestic architecture, admire the works of art, and listen to the sound of the choirs that fill the air. The cathedral welcomes you with open arms, inviting you to discover the beauty and depth of Irish faith.

2.1.2 The Guinness Storehouse

Located in the heart of Dublin, it is one of the most famous and iconic attractions in Ireland. This historic structure, which once housed the warehouses and production facilities of Guinness, is now an interactive museum that celebrates the history and tradition of one of the world's most famous beers.

Upon entering the Guinness Storehouse, you are immediately immersed in a multisensory experience. The tour guides you through a series of interactive exhibits that reveal the secrets of beer production, from the selection of ingredients to fermentation and perfect blending. You can even discover the art of pouring a perfect Guinness, with the opportunity to test your skills at the Guinness Academy.

The Guinness Storehouse also offers a spectacular panoramic view of the city of Dublin from the Gravity Bar, located on the top floor of the building. Here you can enjoy a pint of fresh Guinness, while admiring the enchanting skyline and famous monuments of Dublin.

But the Guinness Storehouse is much more than just a beer museum. It's a place that celebrates the history, culture, and identity of Ireland. During the tour, you will have the opportunity to explore the stories of the people behind Guinness, learn about their dedication and passion for beer, and understand the impact the company has had on the local community over the years.

Whether you are a beer enthusiast or simply interested in Irish culture, the Guinness Storehouse is a must-see during your trip to Dublin. Get ready to immerse yourself in a unique journey into the world of beer, discover the history of an Irish icon, and raise your glass in a toast to the authentic Guinness experience.

2.1.3 The National Museum of Ireland

The National Museum of Ireland, with its locations in Dublin and other cities in Ireland, is a cultural treasure that houses a vast collection of artifacts that tell the history and culture of the country. These museums offer visitors the opportunity to immerse themselves in the past and explore Irish traditions, art, and archaeology.The National Museum in Dublin, located on Kildare Street, hosts a wide range of exhibits that span from prehistoric art, to the Viking age, to the medieval era and beyond. Here you can admire unique treasures such as the famous Ardagh Chalice, the large Broighter Gold Collar, and numerous Celtic artifacts, including jewelry and weapons.The other locations of the National Museum of Ireland include the Museum of Archaeology, the Museum of Natural History, and the Museum of Country Life. The Museum of Archaeology in Dublin is renowned for its collection of ancient artifacts, including skulls and Viking artifacts, while the Museum of Natural History is famous for its vast collection of animals and natural history. The Museum of Country Life, located in Castlebar, County Mayo, offers an immersion in rural and traditional Irish life.

The museums of the National Museum of Ireland are a veritable treasure trove that tell the story of Irish history and culture. With interactive exhibits, permanent and temporary exhibitions, visitors will have the opportunity to delve into the wealth of Ireland's heritage and explore the various facets of its history.Regardless of your interest, the National Museum of Ireland is a must-visit place during your trip to Ireland. You will discover fascinating stories, breathtaking works of art, and a sense of connection with the past that will leave a lasting impression.

2.2 Galway

Overlooking the Atlantic on the west coast of Ireland, Galway is a perfect blend of ancient and modern, traditional culture and vibrant contemporary atmosphere. Renowned for its lively music and arts scene, Galway was designated European Capital of Culture in 2020, a recognition of its cultural richness.

One of the most iconic places in the city is the Latin Quarter area. The cobblestone streets, colorful 17th-century buildings, and numerous pubs and shops make the Latin Quarter the beating heart of Galway. As you stroll, you can watch street performers' shows or stop for a bite at one of the many quality restaurants serving everything from the freshest seafood to fusion cuisine.

Not far from here is the Spanish Arch, one of the few structures remaining from the city's ancient walls. Built in the 16th century, the arch was once part of the city's defense and is now a silent reminder of Galway's rich history.

A walk along Galway Bay is a must for every visitor. The waterfront offers spectacular views of the sea and surrounding hills. On a clear day, it is possible to see the Burren hills to the south and the Connemara mountains to the north. Along the walk, you will also find the famous statue of the girl with the geese, an ode to the city's tradition of raising geese.

Galway is famous for its music, and there's no better place to experience it than in one of its many pubs. From traditional Irish music to modern folk sounds, there's always something playing in town. A trip to Galway wouldn't be complete without spending an evening in one of these pubs, listening to live music and immersing yourself in the atmosphere.

In addition to the city itself, Galway is also an excellent starting point for exploring the wild beauty of Connemara or visiting the Aran Islands, three islands that are bastions of Gaelic culture and language.

Whether you're a history enthusiast, a music lover, a nature explorer, or a foodie, Galway has something to offer everyone. Its fascinating blend of old and new, its creative spirit, and its warm hospitality make it a must-see destination for any trip to Ireland.

2.3 The Giant's Causeway and Antrim Coast

Located on the northern coast of Northern Ireland, the Giant's Causeway is one of the country's most fascinating natural treasures. This UNESCO World Heritage Site is known for its unusual hexagonal basalt formations, created by an ancient volcanic eruption about 60 million years ago.

Local legend, however, tells a different story: the Causeway was built by the Irish giant Fionn mac Cumhaill to challenge his Scottish rival Benandonner. When Benandonner crossed the Causeway to confront Fionn, he was tricked into thinking that Fionn was a much larger giant, and he fled, destroying the Causeway behind him.

Walking along the Causeway is a truly unique experience. The basalt columns form steps leading directly into the sea, creating a truly spectacular landscape. The most famous formations are the 'Giant's Staircase', the 'Bride's Seat', and the "Organ".

But the Giant's Causeway is just the beginning of the journey along the stunning Antrim Coast. This area is famous for its imposing cliffs, sandy beaches, green valleys, and sparkling blue waters. Along the way, you can discover picturesque villages, ancient castles, and breathtaking vistas.

One of the highlights of the trip is the Carrick-a-Rede rope bridge, a suspension bridge 30 meters above the sea that offers incredible views of the coast and the sea. Another point of interest is Dunluce Castle, a 16th-century ruin that sits on a cliff overlooking the sea.

The journey along the Antrim Coast is not just

a trip through beautiful landscapes, but also a journey through history and mythology. Every castle, every village, and every rock has a story to tell, and there is always something new to discover.

Whether you choose to explore on foot, by bike, or by car, the Giant's Causeway and the Antrim Coast offer an unforgettable adventure in the heart of Ireland's wild and enchanting nature. And no matter which story you prefer - that of the giant Fionn or that of the geologists - the Giant's Causeway is a place that is sure to enchant.

To the west of the Giant's Causeway, you'll find the Carrick-a-Rede Rope Bridge, another must-visit site. This rope suspension bridge, originally built by salmon fishermen more than 350 years ago, dramatically sways 30 meters above the rocks and tumultuous waters of the North Irish Sea. If you dare to cross it, you'll be rewarded with spectacular views of the Antrim coast, Rathlin Island, and Scotland.

Continuing along the coast, you'll arrive in

Ballycastle, a charming town that represents the entrance to the Glens of Antrim, nine verdant valleys descending towards the sea. These "glens" are famous for their natural beauty, their babbling rivers, and their spectacular waterfalls.

The Antrim Coast is also known for its wealth of historic castles and manors. One of the most impressive is Dunluce Castle, a towering 16th-century ruin perched on the edge of a cliff directly above the ocean. This castle, which inspired C.S. Lewis to create Cair Paravel Castle in "The Chronicles of Narnia", offers breathtaking views of the North Sea and the Giant's Causeway.

But there's much more to the Antrim Coast than its famous landmarks. Along the way, you'll have the opportunity to explore charming fishing villages, stop in cozy pubs and craft shops, and enjoy the warm and welcoming hospitality for which Ireland is famous.

Another hidden treasure along the Antrim Coast is the Dark Hedges, an 18th-century tree-lined road that became famous for its role in the "Game of Thrones" television series. This stretch of road, lined with twisted beech trees that create a natural tunnel, is a dream for photographers and a magical place to explore.

If you're a golf enthusiast, the Antrim Coast is also home to the Royal Portrush Golf Club, one of the best golf courses in the world and the site of the 2019 Open Championship. Located on a stretch of dunes on the north coast of Northern Ireland, it offers breathtaking views of the ocean.

Finally, make sure you take the time to enjoy the beautiful wildlife along the route. The area is a paradise for birdwatching enthusiasts, with a large variety of seabirds nesting along the cliffs, including fulmars, guillemots, puffins, and cormorants. With a bit of luck, you might also spot dolphins playing in the waves off the coast.

Visiting the Giant's Causeway and the Antrim Coast is a journey into the heart of Northern Ireland's natural beauty, history, and charm.

It's an experience that will leave you speechless and that you will carry in your heart forever.

2.4 Cork and the Ring of Kerry

Cork, Ireland's second-largest city, is a must-visit for every traveler in the southern part of the island. Located on the River Lee, Cork is a vibrant city with a fascinating blend of history and modernity. Its cobblestone streets, historic churches, bustling shopping streets, and numerous restaurants and cafes make it an intriguing place to explore.

In the heart of the city, you'll find St. Patrick's Street, Cork's main shopping artery, lined with shops of every kind. Not far away is the English Market, an indoor market boasting an extraordinary variety of local food products, from meats and cheeses to seafood and sweets.

For history buffs, Cork offers numerous sites of interest, including St. Fin Barre's Cathedral, a magnificent example of neo-Gothic architecture, and Cork City Gaol, a former prison now transformed into a museum that tells the story of prison life in 19th-century Ireland.

Perhaps the greatest attraction of Cork, however, is its access to spectacular Irish countryside. Just a few kilometers from the city, you'll find Blarney Castle, one of Ireland's most famous castles. Here, you can explore the lush castle gardens, admire the imposing structure, and of course, kiss the Blarney Stone to gain the gift of eloquence.

In addition to Blarney, Cork is also the ideal starting point for exploring the Ring of Kerry, one of Ireland's most famous tourist routes. This 179 km loop will take you through some of Ireland's most spectacular landscapes, including mountains, lakes, waterfalls, and the wild Atlantic coast.

The Ring of Kerry offers an abundance of attractions along its path. Visit the town of Killarney and its stunning national park, with its ancient oak forests, enchanting lakes, and imposing 19th-century manor. Take a break in the picturesque town of Kenmare, known for its local craft boutiques, gourmet restaurants, and lively folk music. Or explore Killarney National Park, where you can stroll on the Torc Waterfall or take a horse-drawn carriage tour through the Gap of Dunloe.

The breathtaking beauty of the Ring of Kerry, combined with the vibrant and welcoming atmosphere of Cork, makes this area one of the most beautiful in Ireland. Whether you're a history enthusiast, a nature lover, or just a traveler in search of new adventures, you'll find much to love in this corner of Ireland.

2.5 The Cliffs of Moher

The Cliffs of Moher are one of Ireland's most famous tourist attractions and are an unmissable experience for any visitor. These majestic rock formations rise up to 214 meters above the Atlantic and stretch for 8 kilometers along the western coast of Clare County. The vastness of the cliffs, the incessant rumble of the waves crashing against the rocks, and the sense of infinity you feel looking at the horizon deeply move all those who visit them.

The main attraction is O'Brien's Tower, a stone tower built in the 19th century that offers spectacular views of the cliffs and the ocean. On a clear day, it is possible to see the Aran Islands and the mountains of Connemara. If you are lucky, you might even spot seals, dolphins, or even sharks swimming offshore.

But the Cliffs of Moher are not just a place to admire the view. There are also several hiking trails that wind along the cliffs, offering the opportunity to explore local fauna and flora, including various species of seabirds such as the puffin, the guillemot, and the kittiwake.

Near the cliffs is the Moher Visitor Centre, an underground visitor center built in respect of the surrounding environment. Here, visitors can learn all about the cliffs, their geology, history, and ecological importance through interactive exhibits and films. The center also offers a cafe, a souvenir shop, and visitor facilities.

No matter whether you visit the Cliffs of Moher in the sun, amidst fog, at sunset, or on a stormy day – their wild and majestic beauty is always impressive, and their sight will remain imprinted in your memory for a long time. Be sure to bring a camera to capture the magnificence of this place and, above all, take the time to breathe in the salty air, listen to the sound of the sea, and feel the power of nature surrounding you. It is not just a place to visit, but an experience to live.

2.6 Glendalough Valley

Hidden among the Wicklow Mountains, you will find the Glendalough Valley, a place of extraordinary natural beauty and great historical importance. This glacial valley is famous for its impressive monastic complex, dating back to the time of St. Kevin in the 6th century, and for its two sparkling lakes, from which it takes its name (Glendalough means "valley of the two lakes" in Gaelic).

The monastic complex of Glendalough is one of the best-preserved monastic sites in Ireland. Among its remains stand out the 30-meter high Round Tower, used as a refuge in case of Viking attacks, the Cathedral of St. Peter and St. Paul, and the Church of St. Kevin, known as "St. Kevin's kitchen" due to its unusual bell-shaped roof.

Despite the richness of its history, it is the natural beauty of Glendalough that truly steals the scene. Its two lakes, nestled among hills and forests, offer a panorama of rare beauty. There are numerous hiking trails of varying difficulty that will take you through ancient woods, along sparkling waterways, and overlooking the lakeshores. No matter if you are an experienced hiker or a beginner, you will find a route suitable for you.

Among the natural attractions of Glendalough, the Poulanass waterfall is particularly captivating. This waterfall is fed by mountain waters that rush down the hill, creating a cool and lively stream. The path to the waterfall is an adventure in itself, as it will take you through a beautiful coniferous forest and along the riverbed.

Another highlight of a visit to Glendalough is the local wildlife. With a bit of luck, you might spot red or Sika deer, in addition to an abundance of birds and insects. In the fall, the colors of the landscape become particularly spectacular, with leaves turning into shades of gold, orange, and red.

Visit Glendalough to immerse yourself in Ireland's history, admire its breathtaking landscapes, and enjoy the peace and tranquility of nature. Whether you are a history enthusiast, a nature lover, or a peace seeker, you will find something special in this enchanted valley.

2.7 Donegal and the Wild Atlantic Way

In the remote northwest of Ireland, Donegal is a county of untamed landscapes and wild beauty. With its vast peatlands, its rocky mountains, its jagged cliffs, and its deserted beaches, Donegal is a must-visit destination for those wishing to explore the less tourist-beaten Ireland.

The town of Donegal, with its 15th-century castle and Diamond Square, is a perfect starting point for exploring the county. From here, it is possible to set off for a tour of the Wild Atlantic Way, a scenic road that winds along the western coast of Ireland, from Malin Head in Donegal to Kinsale in Cork.

The Wild Atlantic Way offers breathtaking landscapes at every turn. The Slieve League cliffs, the second highest in Ireland after the Cliffs of Moher, offer breathtaking views of the Atlantic. Glenveagh National Park, the second largest national park in Ireland, hosts a Victorian castle, an ornamental garden, and a population of red deer.

Donegal is also known for its rich culture and musical traditions. You can listen to traditional folk music in many of the county's pubs or participate in one of the many music festivals during the year. And don't miss the opportunity to learn a few words of Gaelic, still widely spoken in some parts of the county.

But perhaps the greatest treasure of Donegal is its people. Known for their warm welcome and their indomitable spirit, the inhabitants of Donegal will make you feel at home. If you want to discover Ireland at its purest, untainted by mass tourism, Donegal is the place for you.

2.8 Killarney National Park

Located in the heart of Kerry, Killarney National Park is a protected area of over 26,000 acres, the first national park established in Ireland. With its majestic mountains, sparkling lakes, vast forests, and rich wildlife, Killarney National Park offers a wonderful natural adventure to visitors of all ages.

The park is famous for its three lakes: Lough Leane, Muckross Lake, and Upper Lake. Surrounded by mountains and forests, these lakes form a landscape of incredible beauty. There are many ways to explore them: on foot, by bike, by carriage, or by boat. Lake cruises are particularly popular and offer a unique perspective on the park.

Another important attraction of Killarney National Park is the Muckross House and Gardens. This imposing Victorian mansion, surrounded by a well-kept garden and a traditional farm, offers a fascinating glimpse into the life of the upper class in the 19th century. Visitors can explore the house, stroll in the garden, or see the farm animals.

Wildlife is an integral part of Killarney National Park. Nature lovers can spot red deer, peregrine falcons, badgers, foxes, and a variety of birds. In autumn, the deer's bellowing is a phenomenon not to be missed.

For the more adventurous, Killarney National Park offers many opportunities for hiking, with routes ranging from easy walks to challenging climbs. The Gap of Dunloe, a mountain pass with spectacular views, and Carrauntoohil, Ireland's highest mountain, are among the most popular destinations.

2.9 The City of Kilkenny

Situated along the banks of the River Nore, in the province of Leinster, Kilkenny is one of Ireland's most enchanting cities. Known as the "marble city" for its shiny black stones used in many of its buildings, Kilkenny is famous for its rich history, vibrant arts scene, and excellent pubs and restaurants.

The historic heart of Kilkenny is dominated by Kilkenny Castle, a magnificent Anglo-Norman fortress built in the 12th century. The perfectly preserved castle offers visitors a journey back in time, with Victorian-styled furnished rooms, an art gallery, and beautiful English-style gardens. The view of the city from the castle's towers is simply breathtaking.

Another historical place of interest is St. Canice's Cathedral, an ancient 13th-century church with a tall round bell tower. You can climb to the top of the bell tower for a panoramic view of the city and the surrounding countryside.

Kilkenny is also a vibrant hub for arts and crafts. The city hosts numerous artist and craftsperson studios, art galleries, and design shops. The Kilkenny Arts Festival, one of Ireland's major cultural events, attracts artists and art enthusiasts from all over the world each year.

Gastronomy is another attraction in Kilkenny. The city offers a variety of high-quality restaurants, cozy pubs, and charming cafes. Don't miss the opportunity to try Kilkenny's traditional red beer in one of the many city pubs.

In short, Kilkenny is a city that offers something for everyone. Whether you're a history lover, an art enthusiast, or a foodie, you'll fall in love with this captivating Irish city.

2.10 Connemara and the Aran Islands

In the northwest corner of County Galway, the region of Connemara is a place of wild natural beauty. Jagged landscapes, enchanted lakes, imposing mountains, and spectacular coastlines make Connemara a true paradise for nature lovers.

Connemara National Park is an ideal starting point for exploring the area. With over 2,000 hectares of mountains, bogs, heathlands, and forests, the park offers a range of hiking trails for all skill levels. Among the local fauna, you might spot the famous Connemara pony, otters, peregrine falcons, and a variety of birds.

The Connemara coast is equally impressive, with a series of deserted beaches, hidden coves, and scattered islands. Dog's Bay and Gurteen Bay beaches are particularly beautiful, with fine white sand and crystal-clear waters.

A few miles off the coast of Connemara are the Aran Islands, a group of three islands that retain a strong sense of Irish tradition. On the largest island, Inishmore, you will find Dun Aonghasa, an ancient fort on the edge of a 100-meter high cliff. A trip to the Aran Islands is like a journey back in time, where Gaelic is still the primary language and life has a slower pace.

Connemara and the Aran Islands offer an authentic Irish experience, away from the crowds of tourists. Whether you're seeking outdoor adventure, ancient history, or simply peace and tranquility, these destinations have a lot to offer.

Continuing the journey in the Connemara region, you cannot miss a visit to the town of Clifden, often described as the "capital" of Connemara. This charming town is known for its colorful pubs, local craft shops, and genuine Irish hospitality. The annual Clifden Arts Festival is a time of great liveliness in town, with music performances, poetry readings, art exhibitions, and more.

If you are a history buff, the Marconi Station, where the first transatlantic radio messages were sent, and the Alcock and Brown Landing Site, where the first nonstop transatlantic flight landed, are must-see destinations.

For fishing enthusiasts, the lakes and rivers of Connemara offer excellent opportunities for trout and salmon fishing. And if you prefer horse riding, there's nothing better than a ride among the Twelve Bens mountains or along the beach.

Finally, a visit to Connemara would not be complete without a tasting of local whiskey. The Connemara Distillery produces the only peated single malt Irish whiskey, famous for its rich and smoky taste.

Connemara and the Aran Islands represent the essence of Ireland: natural beauty, fascinating history, rich culture, and warm and welcoming people. These destinations are a real treasure to discover.

2.10.1 Kylemore Castle

Kylemore Castle, located in the picturesque Connemara region of Ireland, is a wonderful architectural gem that captures the hearts of visitors from all over the world. This enchanting castle, nestled among majestic mountains and overlooking the tranquil Lough Pollacapall, exudes elegance and charm.

Built in the late 19th century, Kylemore Castle

was initially a private residence before being transformed into a Benedictine abbey and later a prestigious boarding school. Today, it stands as a testament to Ireland's rich history and romance. Its fairy-tale structure, with its turrets, protruding arches, and lush gardens, creates an enchanting atmosphere that transports visitors back in time.

Exploring the interior of the castle is like taking a journey into the past. The sumptuously furnished reception rooms, with their intricate woodwork, stained glass windows, and antique furniture, evoke a sense of grandeur and sophistication. The magnificent neo-Gothic chapel, with its intricate details and ethereal atmosphere, is a sight to behold.

Surrounded by beautiful manicured gardens and serene lakes, Kylemore Castle offers a sense of tranquility and natural beauty. Visitors can stroll in the Victorian walled garden, filled with vibrant flowers and tranquil ponds, or take a walk along the lakeshore, enjoying the breathtaking reflections of the castle on the water.

Whether you are an architecture enthusiast, a history buff, or simply seeking a peaceful escape in nature, Kylemore Castle will capture your imagination and leave a lasting impression. Its timeless beauty and serene surroundings make it a must-visit destination in Ireland, offering a glimpse into the romantic past of this enchanting country.

CHAPTER 3: Irish Gastronomy

3.1 Introduction to Irish Cuisine

Irish cuisine is a journey of simple but memorable flavors that reflect the lush terrain and rich agricultural tradition of the island. With a temperate climate that promotes the growth of green grass all year round, Ireland is blessed with forage-fed sheep and cows that produce top-quality meat and dairy. The fertile soil provides a generous variety of vegetables, while the clean rivers and the Atlantic Ocean yield an abundant harvest of fish and seafood.

One of the main characteristics of Irish cuisine is the use of simple and fresh ingredients. Potatoes, cabbage, carrots, peas, and onions are some of the most common vegetables used in traditional dishes. Lamb, beef, and pork are the main meats, while salmon, cod, and oysters are favorites for fish dishes.

Ireland is famous for its artisan cheeses, with over 50 different types produced across the country. Cashel Blue, Gubbeen, Coolea, and

Milleens are just a few examples of the delicious cheeses you can enjoy during your trip.

Finally, the culture of Irish pubs adds another distinctive element to the country's cuisine. In addition to the famous Guinness and other craft beers, in pubs, you can enjoy traditional dishes such as Irish Stew, Bangers and Mash (sausages and mashed potatoes), and Fish and Chips, all accompanied by live music and a welcoming atmosphere.

In essence, Irish cuisine is an expression of its people: warm, welcoming, and generous. Prepare to immerse yourself in a culinary experience that will satisfy not only your palate but also your soul.

3.2 Irish Stew

One of the most emblematic dishes of Irish cuisine is the Irish Stew. This is a hearty and traditional dish, perfect for warming up on cold winter days or for enjoying comfort food at any time of the year.

In its most traditional form, the Irish Stew

consists of a handful of simple but tasty ingredients: lamb or mutton, potatoes, onions, and carrots. Some variations may also include celery, parsley, and barley. The meat, usually cut into pieces, is slowly cooked with the vegetables in a broth until it becomes tender and juicy.

The Irish Stew is a humble dish, born out of the necessity to create a substantial meal with few available ingredients. However, its strength lies in its simplicity. The slow cooking time allows the flavors to meld together, creating a dish with a rich and deep taste. The potatoes partially break down during cooking, thickening the broth and giving it a creamy consistency.

You can find Irish Stew in almost all pubs and restaurants in Ireland, each with its slightly different version. No matter where you try it, the Irish Stew will make you feel as if you are sitting next to a cozy fire, enjoying true Irish hospitality.

Tasting Irish Stew is not just a meal, but a culinary experience that brings you closer to

Irish culture and history. So, the next time you're in Ireland, make sure to make room for a plate of this warm and comforting stew.

The essence of Irish Stew is its rustic nature and the use of fresh and local ingredients. The lamb or mutton used in the stew often comes from sheep raised on Irish green pastures, which gives the meat a distinct and delicious flavor. The vegetables are typically grown in local gardens, while herbs such as thyme, sage, and parsley, often added to flavor the stew, are picked fresh.

It's interesting to note that Irish Stew is also a versatile dish. While lamb is the most traditional ingredient, it is also possible to use beef or even chicken. Moreover, some variations of the stew even include seafood, like mussels, giving rise to a completely new and equally tasty dish.

Although it is a traditional dish, the Irish Stew is continuously evolving, with modern cooks reinterpreting it in new and interesting ways. Some may add non-traditional ingredients, like beets or mushrooms, to give a contemporary touch to the dish. Others may serve it with homemade soda bread, to soak up the tasty broth.

In any case, the Irish Stew remains a pillar of Irish cuisine, a symbol of the country's connection with the land, and a testament to its tradition of homemade comfort food. There is nothing better than enjoying a steaming plate of Irish Stew after a day spent exploring the wonders of Ireland.

3.3 Colcannon

Colcannon is another classic dish you will find on the table in many Irish homes, especially during Halloween and St. Patrick's Day celebrations. This creamy side dish is a triumph of rustic flavors, combining mashed potatoes with cabbage or kale, onions or leeks, butter, and sometimes smoked bacon.

The beauty of Colcannon lies in its simplicity. The potatoes, which are a staple ingredient in Irish cuisine, are boiled until soft, then mashed and mixed with lightly cooked cabbage and a generous dose of butter. The result is a dish with a rich, earthy flavor, and a velvety texture that melts in your mouth.

In the Halloween tradition, a ring or a coin was often inserted into the Colcannon - it was said that whoever found it would have good luck for the coming year. Furthermore, Irish families often leave a portion of Colcannon with extra butter on the window as an offering for wandering ghosts - a testament to the deep bond between this dish and Irish folk traditions.

Although often seen as a simple side dish, Colcannon can be enriched with pieces of sausage or bacon to become a main dish. It's also delicious served alongside a roast or a slice of smoked salmon.

If you visit Ireland, be sure to taste Colcannon in an authentic Irish pub or local restaurant. Not only will it delight you with its comforting and familiar flavor, but it will also give you a taste of Ireland's rural roots and rich traditions.3.4 Oysters

Ireland, with its cold and clean waters, is famous for its high-quality oysters. Whether you're a seafood enthusiast or a novice, you can't visit Ireland without trying its fresh oysters, known for their rich and distinctive flavor.

Oysters are served in various ways in Ireland. The most traditional is simply raw, often with a squeeze of lemon or a bit of tabasco sauce. The experience of eating a raw oyster is unique: the briny taste of the sea, the fleshy texture, and the slight sweetness of the oyster come together to create a truly memorable culinary experience.

In addition to raw oysters, you might find grilled or baked oysters, often topped with cheese, bacon, or garlic. These variations offer a different experience, with the oyster becoming more fleshy and flavorful.

Ireland also hosts several oyster festivals throughout the year, the most famous of which is the Galway Oyster Festival. This annual event celebrates the oyster season with tastings, oyster opening competitions, and, of course, plenty of pints of Guinness.

Irish oysters are much more than a dish; they are a symbol of the country's connection to the sea and a culinary tradition that dates back hundreds of years. Whether you decide to taste them in a luxury restaurant, a cozy country pub, or a lively festival, oysters offer an unparalleled taste of Ireland.

3.4 Oysters

Ireland, with its cold and clean waters, is famous for its high-quality oysters. Whether you're a seafood enthusiast or a novice, you can't visit Ireland without trying its fresh oysters, known for their rich and distinctive flavor.

Oysters are served in various ways in Ireland. The most traditional is simply raw, often with a squeeze of lemon or a bit of tabasco sauce. The experience of eating a raw oyster is unique: the briny taste of the sea, the fleshy texture, and the slight sweetness of the oyster come together to create a truly memorable culinary experience.

In addition to raw oysters, you might find grilled or baked oysters, often topped with cheese, bacon, or garlic. These variations offer a different experience, with the oyster becoming more fleshy and flavorful.

Ireland also hosts several oyster festivals throughout the year, the most famous of which is the Galway Oyster Festival. This annual event celebrates the oyster season with tastings, oyster opening competitions, and, of course, plenty of pints of Guinness.

Irish oysters are much more than a dish; they are a symbol of the country's connection to the sea and a culinary tradition that dates back hundreds of years. Whether you decide to taste them in a luxury restaurant, a cozy country pub, or a lively festival, oysters offer an unparalleled taste of Ireland.

3.5 Guinness

Guinness is undoubtedly the most iconic alcoholic beverage associated with Ireland. This stout beer is renowned worldwide for its distinctive dark color, rich and complex flavor, and dense, creamy foam.

The history of Guinness dates back to 1759, when Arthur Guinness founded the brewery in Dublin. Since then, Guinness has become a true symbol of Irish identity and its pub culture. It is a beer loved and drunk by both the Irish and visitors from all over the world.

The production of Guinness requires skill and patience. The malted barley is roasted at a high temperature, giving the beer its characteristic dark color and a toasted, slightly bitter flavor. The fermentation process occurs with the addition of special yeast, known as "Guinness yeast," which helps create the distinctive effervescence and rounded taste of the beer.

While you can enjoy a Guinness in any Irish pub, we recommend visiting the Guinness Storehouse in Dublin. This famous tourist attraction is located in the former Guinness factory and offers an interactive experience that guides you through the history, production, and unique taste of this beer.

Sipping a Guinness in an authentic Irish pub is much more than a simple act of tasting. It's a social experience, a way to immerse yourself in Irish culture, listen to traditional music, and share stories with friends or locals. So, if you find yourself in an Irish pub, don't forget to raise your glass and toast with a pint of Guinness, a true symbol of Ireland.

Guinness also has a series of events and celebrations tied to its culture and tradition. One of the most notable events is Saint Patrick's Day, the Irish national holiday held on March 17th each year. During this festive day, pubs throughout the country are filled with music, dancing, singing, and laughter as people raise their glass of Guinness to celebrate Irish pride.

In addition to Saint Patrick's Day, Guinness also has a tradition called "Arthur's Day" held every year in September. This event commemorates the founder of Guinness, Arthur Guinness, and celebrates the beer's legacy and success. On this day, pubs host live concerts and offer special promotions on Guinness, creating a festive atmosphere throughout the country.

If you're a beer enthusiast, we also recommend visiting Dublin's historic pubs, like the famous "The Brazen Head" or "The Guinness Storehouse Gravity Bar". These places offer an authentic experience where you can immerse yourself in Irish beer culture and savor a fresh Guinness, served to perfection.

Guinness is much more than just a beer: it represents Irish history, tradition, and conviviality. It's a drink to be savored slowly, allowing its unique flavors to expand on the palate and giving a sense of fulfillment and connection to the rich Irish heritage. Whether you're a beer expert or a novice, you can't leave Ireland without tasting a pint of

Guinness and raising your glass for a warm "Sláinte!" (Cheers!)

3.6 Where to Find the Best Local Cuisine

Ireland is renowned for its homestyle cooking and fresh, quality ingredients. Finding the best local cuisine means immersing yourself in traditional pubs, high-quality restaurants, and rural locations that value local produce and Irish culinary traditions.

A great starting point for discovering Irish cuisine is Dublin, Ireland's vibrant capital. Here you will find a wide range of restaurants serving traditional dishes with a modern twist. The Temple Bar neighborhood is renowned for its cozy pubs and restaurants offering dishes like Irish Stew, Roast Beef, and Fish and Chips, accompanied by a pint of Guinness.

If you are looking for authenticity, head to the rural regions of Ireland. Along the western coast, you will find small pubs and restaurants offering freshly caught fish and super fresh seafood. In County Cork, you can savor delicious local cheeses and high-quality meat dishes. The Kerry region is renowned for its lamb and the famous "Ring of Kerry," where you can taste authentic local specialties.

The cities of Galway, Cork, Limerick, and Belfast are other places to find a vibrant food scene. Here you will find restaurants serving contemporary and creative dishes, using local and seasonal ingredients. Don't miss the opportunity to try dishes like Burren Smoked Salmon, Irish Soda Bread, Boxty (a kind of potato pancake), and Black Pudding.

Additionally, exploring local markets is a fantastic way to discover Irish cuisine. Markets like the English Market in Cork and St. George's Market in Belfast offer a wide selection of fresh produce, artisan cheeses, freshly baked bread, traditional sweets, and more.

The search for the best local cuisine in Ireland is a culinary adventure that will lead you to discover the country's traditions, flavors, and passion. Be curious, try new dishes, and let yourself be carried away by the warm welcome that only Ireland can offer.

CHAPTER 4: Local history

4.1 The Celts and Irish Culture

Ireland has a rich Celtic heritage that has profoundly influenced its culture, language, and traditions. The Celts arrived on the island around 500 BC, coming from the region of Central Europe. Their presence has left an indelible imprint on Ireland's history.

The Irish Celts were an agricultural and warrior people, divided into tribes with a complex social structure. They believed in a series of pagan deities and practiced religious rites involving sacrifices and sacred ceremonies. The figure of the druid, a Celtic priest and scholar, was of great importance in Celtic society, as they were responsible for spirituality, education, and law.

Celtic culture was expressed through music, art, and poetry. Traditional Irish music has deep roots in the Celtic tradition, with instruments such as the fiddle, the tin whistle, the harp, and the bodhrán creating enchanting melodies. Celtic art is characterized by intricate motifs, with knots, spirals, and interlaces representing the connection between the natural world and the divine. Poetry was highly valued, with bards preserving and passing on the stories and wisdom of the people.

The Celtic language, known as Irish Gaelic or simply Irish, is still spoken in some parts of Ireland and represents a symbol of cultural identity. In recent decades, there has been a renewed interest in promoting the Irish language and culture, with initiatives to teach Irish in schools and promote its use in daily life.

Despite the influence of other peoples and cultures over the centuries, Celtic culture has maintained its strength and vitality in Ireland. Celebrations like the Samhain festival (the ancient Celtic feast that gave rise to modern Halloween) and the love for traditional stories, music, and folklore are testament to the Celtic heritage that still permeates Irish life today. Exploring Celtic culture means immersing oneself in a world of mystery, spirituality, and beauty that has left an indelible mark on Ireland's history.

4.2 The Viking Invasion

In the 8th century, Ireland witnessed the invasion of the Vikings, warriors and navigators from Scandinavian countries. These bold explorers, known for their skill in maritime navigation, made landfall along the Irish coasts and founded permanent settlements.

One of the primary targets of the Vikings was the island of Lindisfarne, located off the northeastern coast of England, which they sacked in 793 AD. This event marked the beginning of the Viking raids in the British Isles, which quickly extended to Ireland.

The Vikings established settlements called "longphorts" along the Irish coasts, using them as bases for their trade and military operations. Among the main Viking settlements in Ireland were Dublin (founded around 841 AD), Waterford, Wexford, and Limerick.

The Viking influence in Ireland was significant. The Vikings introduced new shipbuilding techniques, such as the construction of longships, fast and maneuverable vessels, which facilitated maritime trade. These Viking settlements became important commercial centers and exchange points between Ireland and other Viking regions.

Beyond the military and commercial aspect, the Vikings also influenced Irish culture. They introduced new elements into the language, architecture, and art. For example, Viking influence can be noted in the architecture of "round tower" style churches and in the interlaced decorative motifs found in objects and manuscripts.

Despite initial clashes, the Vikings gradually integrated into Irish society. Through mixed marriages and mutual cultural adaptations, a sort of fusion was created between Viking traditions and Irish ones.

The Viking invasion had a lasting impact on Irish history and culture. While the Vikings represent a period of conflict and looting, they also helped to transform Ireland into a hub of commercial and cultural exchanges in the broader context of the Viking world. The Viking legacy can still be seen and appreciated in places like Dublin, with its Viking heritage bearing witness to the influence of this population in Ireland's history.

4.3 The Norman Era and the Kingdom of Ireland

In the 12th century, Ireland was invaded by the Normans, led by King Henry II of England. The Norman invasion marked another significant chapter in Irish history, leading to substantial political, social, and cultural transformations.

King Henry II aimed to establish English control over Ireland and introduce a more organized administrative structure. The Normans, with their army and advanced military technology, quickly managed to conquer numerous cities and regions of Ireland. Among these, Dublin became the Norman capital and a significant center of power.

Under Norman rule, the "Kingdom of Ireland" was established, with an Anglo-Norman ruling class and a subject Irish population. The Normans introduced a feudal system, based on land ownership in exchange for military services and other duties.

The Normans also built numerous castles and fortifications throughout the country, with the aim of protecting their power and maintaining control over the Irish territory. These castles, still visible today, are a significant historical heritage and bear witness to Norman influence on Irish architecture and society.

While the Normans had a dominant presence on the island, Ireland remained divided between the regions under English control and those still governed by local Irish chieftains. This led to centuries of conflicts between English forces and Irish populations seeking to defend their autonomy.

Despite the tensions, important institutions were initiated during the Norman period that had a lasting impact on Ireland. The City of Dublin was founded, the first universities were established, and legal reforms were introduced. The Norman influence also affected the Irish language and culture, contributing to a certain fusion between the Anglo-Norman and Irish traditions. The Norman era in Ireland lasted several centuries, but English influence intensified over the subsequent centuries. The Kingdom of Ireland was gradually integrated into the United Kingdom in 1801, paving the way for new chapters of Irish history that would develop over the following centuries.

4.4 English Domination and the Great Famine

From the 16th to the 19th century, Ireland underwent a period of English domination that had profound consequences on its history and the lives of its population. During this period, Ireland was subjected to oppressive policies, resource exploitation, and systemic discrimination.

English domination intensified, particularly from the 16th century, when King Henry VIII sought to extend his control over Ireland. This period is characterized by colonization and the confiscation of Irish lands by English settlers, while the Irish population was often deprived of their lands and resources.

Discrimination and oppression also manifested through penal laws that imposed restrictions on Irish Catholics and promoted the settlement of English Protestants on the island. These policies aimed to undermine Irish culture and religion, seeking to assimilate the Irish population to English identity and language.

A pivotal event that deeply marked the history of Ireland during this period was the Great Famine, also known as the Great Potato Famine, which struck Ireland between 1845 and 1852. The Great Famine was caused by the spread of a fungal disease that destroyed potato crops, which were the staple food of the Irish population.

The famine led to a severe shortage of food, causing the death of over a million people due to hunger and related diseases, and forcing millions of Irish people to emigrate in search of a better life. This tragic event had lasting social and economic consequences on Ireland, with entire communities devastated and an irreparable loss of culture and population.

English domination and the Great Famine deeply marked Ireland and its national identity. However, these hardships also fueled a sense of pride and the fight for independence that will characterize the next chapter of Irish history.

4.5 The Fight for Independence and Modern Ireland

The 20th century was a period of significant transformations for Ireland, characterized by the struggle for independence from British rule and the creation of a sovereign state. This historical phase defined modern Ireland and shaped the country's national identity.

The struggle for independence began to take shape at the beginning of the 20th century, with a nationalist movement seeking political autonomy from the British Empire. Key figures like Charles Stewart Parnell and Michael Collins emerged as charismatic and influential leaders in the pursuit of independence.

One of the pivotal moments was Easter 1916,

when the Irish republican movement, led by the Irish Republican Brotherhood, rebelled against British rule. Although the rebellion was suppressed by British forces, the event marked the beginning of a broader independence movement and inspired further efforts to achieve independence.

After years of struggles, negotiations, and conflicts, the Anglo-Irish Treaty was signed in 1921. This agreement established the Irish Free State, an independent nation with limited autonomy, and created Northern Ireland, which remained part of the United Kingdom. The agreement, however, did not fully satisfy all the desires of the entire independence movement, leading to internal divisions and tensions.

The creation of the Irish Free State marked the beginning of a new era for the country. An autonomous government was established and initiatives were undertaken to promote Irish identity, culture, and language. However, the division of Ireland and the issue of Northern Ireland remained a source of tension and conflict for subsequent decades, culminating in the period known as "The Troubles", a phase of political violence and community clashes in the 1960s, 70s, and 80s.

In recent decades, a peace and reconciliation process has led to a relaxation of tensions in Northern Ireland. In 1998, the Good Friday Agreement was signed, officially ending "The Troubles" and establishing a shared power political structure between unionists and nationalists. This agreement led to greater political stability in Northern Ireland and a period of relative calm.

Meanwhile, the Irish Free State, which assumed the name Republic of Ireland in 1937, followed an independent path. The country developed a parliamentary democracy, achieved significant economic growth, and established itself as a member of the European Union.

Modern Ireland is characterized by a deep sense of national pride, a vibrant culture, and a commitment to peace and prosperity. The Irish identity is evident in the Gaelic language, musical traditions, literature, art, and celebrations such as Saint Patrick's Day, which reflect the richness and diversity of Irish culture.

21st-century Ireland continues to be a rapidly evolving country, facing economic, social, and environmental challenges. However, its history of struggle for independence and its resilience as a nation have laid the groundwork for a future of hope and progress.

CHAPTER 5: Culture and Traditions

5.1 Holidays such as Saint Patrick's Day

Saint Patrick's Day, or the Feast of Saint Patrick, is one of the most important and recognizable holidays in Ireland. Every year, on March 17th, the streets fill with colors, music, dances, and celebrations in honor of Saint Patrick, the patron saint of Ireland.

Saint Patrick's Day celebrations take place not only throughout Ireland but also in many parts of the world, as Irish heritage has widely spread due to immigration. It's a day when the entire Irish community, as well as those who love and appreciate Irish culture, come together to celebrate.

The celebrations are characterized by colorful and vibrant parades that traverse the streets of cities and towns. Saint Patrick's Day parades are famous for their allegorical floats, spectacular costumes, and traditional dances. People wear green clothes, the symbolic color of Ireland, and accessories like top hats, shamrocks, and horseshoe-shaped pins.

Traditional Irish music, with its engaging sounds, is a constant presence during Saint Patrick's Day celebrations. Bands of musicians perform on the streets, in pubs, and in venues specially set up for the occasion, creating a festive and engaging atmosphere. Traditional Irish instruments, like the fiddle, the tin whistle, the bodhrán, and the harp, bring to life cheerful melodies that invite everyone to dance and sing.

During Saint Patrick's Day, pubs come alive with people enjoying the company of friends, drinking a beer, or a glass of Irish whiskey. Guinness, one of the world's most famous beers, is an Irish icon and often raised as a symbol of celebration during this holiday.

Saint Patrick's Day celebrations also offer the opportunity to discover and appreciate Irish culinary traditions. Dishes like Irish Stew, Colcannon (mashed potatoes and cabbage), Boxty (potato pancake), and irresistible soda bread are just some of the delicacies that can be enjoyed on this special day.

Saint Patrick's Day is much more than a simple holiday. It's an occasion to celebrate Irish identity, to honor cultural heritage, and to show the entire world the love and pride for Ireland. It's a day when music, dance, food, and traditions blend to create an atmosphere of joy and belonging, uniting people in a warm embrace of friendship and celebration.

5.2 Legends of the Leprechaun

Leprechaun legends are a fascinating part of Irish culture. These mysterious creatures of folklore are depicted as small elves or gnomes, dressed elegantly with a top hat, short trousers, buckled shoes, and an apron.

According to legend, leprechauns are known to be skilled smiths and keepers of hidden treasure. Their treasure is said to be buried in a pot of gold that is concealed in secret locations like at the foot of a rainbow or at the root of a tree. It is said that if one manages to capture a leprechaun, they will grant a wish in exchange for their freedom.

Leprechauns are playful and cunning creatures. They are said to love playing pranks and can deceive anyone trying to find their treasure. If one manages to capture a leprechaun, it's important to be careful because they can be crafty and attempt to trick their captors.

Leprechaun legends are still very present in Irish culture and images of these captivating creatures can be found in various forms of art and craft. It is common to find representations of leprechauns in jewelry, sculptures, paintings, and traditional craft items.

Leprechauns have become an iconic symbol of Ireland and are often associated with Saint

Patrick's Day and luck. During celebrations, it's common to see people wearing top hats and leprechaun costumes, creating a playful and festive atmosphere.

Leprechaun legends are a testament to the imagination and enchantment that permeate Irish culture. These captivating stories add a touch of mystery and magic to the rich tradition of Irish folklore, helping to preserve the cultural identity of the Irish people through generations.

5.3 Folk Music

Irish folk music is a central element of Irish culture and has a unique charm that has won the hearts of people all over the world. Characterized by lively melodies, catchy rhythms, and moving lyrics, Irish folk music has a long history that traces its roots back in time.

Traditional instruments used in Irish folk music include the fiddle (violin), the tin whistle (metal flute), the bodhrán (frame drum), the acoustic guitar, the Celtic harp, and the banjo. Each instrument contributes to creating the distinctive sound of Irish folk music, with the fiddle often leading the main melody and the tin whistle adding melodic sweetness.

Irish ballads are a fundamental element of folk music. These songs tell stories of love, betrayals, emigration, battles, and the daily life of the Irish people. Irish ballads are characterized by lyrics rich in poetic imagery, evoking feelings of nostalgia, melancholy, and hope.

A unique aspect of Irish folk music is its ability to engage the audience. During sessions of traditional Irish music, people gather in pubs or public spaces to play and sing together. These sessions are often informal and open to anyone who wishes to participate. It's an opportunity to share a passion for music, unite in harmony, and create an atmosphere of festivity and conviviality.

Irish folk music has influenced many musical genres worldwide, such as country and bluegrass. Irish artists like The Dubliners, The Chieftains, Planxty, Clannad, and Sinead O'Connor have brought Irish folk music to the international spotlight, helping to spread the beauty and depth of this musical tradition.

In addition to its presence in live music sessions, Irish folk music is often performed at shows and music festivals. Festivals like the Fleadh Cheoil, which is held annually in various Irish cities, offer the opportunity to fully immerse oneself in folk music, with concerts, competitions, and workshops.

Irish folk music is much more than just a form of entertainment. It is a reflection of the soul and history of the Irish people, a means through which traditions, stories, and emotions of the past are preserved. Irish folk music continues to be loved and appreciated for its beauty, vitality, and its ability to connect people through the universal language of music.

5.4 Gaelic Language

The Irish Gaelic language, or simply Irish, has a long history that traces its roots back to the ancient Celtic traditions of Ireland. It is one of the official languages of Ireland and is considered a vital part of Irish culture and identity.

Irish is a Celtic language belonging to the Goidelic language family. It is one of the oldest languages in Europe and boasts a rich literary tradition dating back centuries. Numerous literary works, poems, and songs have been written in Irish, contributing to its cultural importance.

Despite the influence of English rule over the centuries, the Gaelic language has survived thanks to the efforts of those who preserved and promoted it. Today, there are initiatives aimed at encouraging the use and learning of Irish, especially in the Gaeltacht regions, where Irish is still widely spoken.

Irish schools offer instruction in Irish as part of the curriculum and institutions have been established to promote the language, such as Oireachtas na Gaeilge, an organization that supports and celebrates Irish through cultural events and language competitions.

The Irish Gaelic language has a unique beauty and musicality. Its rules of pronunciation and grammar may seem complex to those unfamiliar with the language, but learning Irish offers an opportunity to immerse oneself in the rich culture and tradition of Ireland.

Irish has a significant impact on the culture and daily life of Ireland. Many place names, family names, and specific terms are of Irish origin. Furthermore, many Irish expressions and idioms find their true meaning only in the Gaelic language, thus revealing the depth and richness of Irish cultural identity.

The Irish Gaelic language is much more than just a means of communication. It represents a direct link with the history, poetry, music, and age-old traditions of Ireland. It is an important cultural resource that is revitalizing its presence in Ireland's contemporary life, offering a precious connection to the country's deep roots and unique identity.

5.5 Literature

Irish literature boasts an ancient and rich tradition, with works ranging from Celtic mythology to modern contemporary novels. Great Irish writers have left an indelible mark on world literature, creating works that tackle universal themes with a unique perspective and poetic language.

Irish literature traces its roots back to ancient sagas and Celtic myths, like the Ulster Cycle and the Fenian Cycle. These stories tell of heroes, battles, love, and magic, and have shaped the worldview of the ancient Irish.

One of the most celebrated Irish authors is Jonathan Swift, known for his satirical novel "Gulliver's Travels," published in 1726. This work, besides being a fantastic adventure, offers a sharp critique of society and political power at the time.

Another great name in Irish literature is Oscar Wilde, famous for his satirical wit and sophisticated style. Works like "The Picture of Dorian Gray" and "The Importance of Being Earnest" showcase Wilde's talent in combining irony and thematic depth.

A cornerstone of Irish literature is undoubtedly James Joyce, author of masterpieces like "Ulysses" and "Dubliners." His complex and experimental writing redefined the form of the modern novel, exploring themes such as identity, history, and the human condition.

Another Nobel laureate in literature from Ireland was Samuel Beckett, known for his innovative plays like "Waiting for Godot" and "Endgame." His writing addresses the absurdity of human existence and the meaning of life in a senseless world.

Irish literature has also been influenced by the country's long poetic tradition. Poets such as W.B. Yeats, Seamus Heaney, and Eavan Boland have left an indelible mark with their poems that tackle themes like love, nature, politics, and identity.

Ireland is also known for its storytelling tradition. Tales and legends passed down orally for generations have been collected and transcribed, thereby preserving a wealth of narratives that reflect the culture and history of the Irish people.

Irish literature is a treasure of creativity, imagination, and introspection. Through the words of its writers, Irish literature offers a window onto the cultural richness of the country and the complexity of its identity. It is an invitation to explore imaginary worlds and to reflect on the human condition, as we immerse ourselves in the wonderful universe of Irish literature.

5.6 Irish Dance

Irish dance is a fascinating and dynamic art form that has deep roots in Irish culture. With its rapid steps, contagious energy, and rhythmic precision, Irish dance has captivated audiences worldwide.

One of the most well-known forms of Irish dance is riverdance. This dance style is characterized by synchronized, fast foot movements, accompanied by upright body postures and arms firmly along the sides. Riverdance gained popularity due to its spectacular theatrical performances, where dancers perform complex steps with great skill and grace.

Another traditional form of Irish dance is set dancing. This group dance involves couples moving together following predefined choreographic figures. Set dancing is a form of social dance that is still practiced today in many Irish rural communities during traditional celebrations and festivals.

Irish dance has evolved over the centuries but has maintained its traditional essence. It's an art form that brings together music, rhythm, and movement in a single thrilling performance.

An iconic element of Irish dance is tap dancing. This dance style focuses on the rhythmic sound created by the heels and toes of the shoes striking the floor. Tap dancers perform fast, synchronized movements, creating a melody with their feet that blends with traditional Irish music.

Irish dance has a strong presence in competitions, especially in feiseanna, the events dedicated to traditional Irish dances. Dancers compete in various categories, showcasing their technical skill and mastery of traditional dances.

The importance of Irish dance in Irish culture is also evident during St. Patrick's Day celebrations and other traditional holidays.

Parades, performances, and Irish dance competitions are central elements of these celebrations, providing an opportunity to showcase the dancers' skills and the contagious energy of the dance.

Irish dance is not just an art form, but also a form of cultural identity. Through dance, tradition is preserved and the love for Irish.

CHAPTER 6: Travel Advice

6.1 The Best Time to Visit Ireland

Ireland is a delightful country to visit at any time of year, but the weather can vary significantly depending on the season. Therefore, choosing the best time to visit depends on your personal preferences and the activities you want to do during your trip.

Summer, from June to August, is considered high season in Ireland. During this period, the weather is generally milder and temperatures range from 15 to 20 degrees Celsius. The days are longer, allowing you to make the most of outdoor activities and explore the charming cities and Irish coast. However, it is important to keep in mind that summer is also the busiest time, especially in major tourist destinations like Dublin, the Antrim Coast, and the Cliffs of Moher. Booking in advance is recommended to ensure accommodations and travel services.

Spring, from March to May, is another good

season to visit Ireland. During this period, temperatures start to rise and vegetation wakes up after the winter. It is an ideal time to explore blooming gardens and enjoy a pleasant walk along the coastal paths. In this season, tourist destinations may be less crowded than in summer, allowing you to enjoy a quieter atmosphere.

Autumn, from September to November, offers spectacular landscapes thanks to the bright colors of the leaves falling from the trees. It is a period when you can experience the magical atmosphere of Irish forests and parks, as well as participate in autumn festivals and cultural events. Temperatures can be cooler than in summer, but still pleasant for outdoor activities. Autumn is also a good time to visit rural regions and immerse yourself in traditional Irish life.

Winter, from December to February, is characterized by colder temperatures and frequent rain. However, Ireland has a unique charm during this season, especially during the Christmas holidays. Cities are decorated with lights and ornaments, and there are numerous Christmas markets and concerts throughout the country. Irish Christmas traditions, such as candlelight processions and traditional music concerts, offer an authentic experience. In addition, winter is a less crowded period, allowing you to enjoy attractions and services with fewer tourists.

Ultimately, Ireland has a unique charm in every season, so choosing the best time depends on your personal preferences. Regardless of the season chosen, be prepared to experience the warm welcome of the Irish, the rich culture, and the natural beauty of the country.

6.2 Transportation

To get around in Ireland, you will have several transportation options at your disposal. Here are some useful information:

Public Transport: The public transport system in Ireland is well developed, with trains and buses connecting the main cities and smaller urban centers. Trains are run by Irish Rail, while buses are operated by several companies, including Bus Éireann. These services offer a convenient and reliable way to get around the country, with links between the main cities and many tourist sites. It is advisable to check the schedules in advance and plan your trip based on your destinations.

Car Rental: If you want to explore Ireland independently and have maximum flexibility, car rental might be the best choice. There are several car rental companies available at airports and in major cities. Driving in Ireland can be a beautiful experience, with scenic roads running through breathtaking landscapes. Remember that in Ireland you drive on the left and roads can be narrow and winding, especially in rural areas. Make sure you familiarize yourself with the local road rules before setting off.

Rental Bikes: In some cities, like Dublin and Cork, there are also electric bike or scooter rental services available to visitors. These means of transport can be a practical and eco-friendly option for getting around in urban areas and visiting points of interest. Make sure you know the local rules for using bicycles and scooters and always respect road safety.

Organized Tours: If you prefer to rely on a travel agency or participate in organized tours, there are many options available to explore Ireland. The tours can cover different regions of the country, giving you the opportunity to visit the main attractions and learn about Irish culture and history through expert guides. Check the details of the tour, such as the itinerary, duration, included transport, and spoken languages, to choose the one that best suits your needs.

Regardless of the method of transport chosen, remember to plan ahead and take into account distances and travel times. Ireland is a relatively small country, but travel time can vary depending on the roads and traffic conditions. Enjoy your trip and discover the beauties of Ireland in all its magnificence!

6.3 What to Pack

When preparing your suitcase for a trip to Ireland, it's important to be prepared for the weather changes and the activities you plan to do during your stay. Here are some essential items to consider:

Clothing layers: Ireland has variable weather, so it's advisable to bring clothing suitable for different weather conditions. Include lightweight sweaters, short and long-sleeved t-shirts, comfortable pants, and a pair of jeans. Make sure you also have a sweater or fleece for cooler days, especially if you visit Ireland outside of summer.

Raincoat or umbrella: Ireland is known for its occasional rain, so it's advisable to bring a lightweight raincoat or foldable umbrella in your suitcase. This will help you stay dry during rainy days and continue to enjoy your outdoor activities.

Comfortable shoes: Expect to do a lot of walking and hiking during your trip to Ireland, so make sure to bring comfortable and sturdy shoes. A pair of hiking shoes or boots are ideal for tackling rough terrain or longer hikes. Make sure to also bring a pair of comfortable shoes for city visits or for more casual evenings.

Outdoor activity clothing: If you plan to explore the Irish countryside or do outdoor activities, such as hiking or cycling, make sure to bring suitable clothing. This might include sturdy pants, a lightweight windproof jacket, and a scarf or hat to protect you from the wind.

Power adapter: Ireland uses the three-pin type G socket, so if you're coming from a country with different sockets, make sure to bring a power adapter to be able to charge your electronic devices during your stay.

Travel towels: Some accommodations may not provide towels, so it's useful to bring along a lightweight, compact travel towel.

Travel accessories: Don't forget to include essential travel accessories like a toiletry bag, a first aid kit, a reusable water bottle, a camera or a phone with photographic capability, and a hat to protect you from the sun.

Consider the season and specific activities you have planned during your trip. For example, if you're visiting Ireland in winter, you might want to bring a heavier coat and a pair of gloves and a hat to protect yourself from the cold.

Remember to limit the amount of luggage you bring with you and respect the airlines' weight limits. Ireland offers self-service laundries and dry cleaning services in major cities, so you can wash your clothes during your stay if necessary.

By packing a suitable suitcase, you will be ready to fully enjoy your adventure in Ireland, remaining comfortable and adapting to the different weather conditions you might encounter.

6.4 Local Norms and Customs to Respect

During your visit to Ireland, it's important to respect local norms and customs to fully immerse yourself in the culture and social fabric of the country. Here are some aspects to keep in mind:

Greetings and courtesy: In Ireland, it's common to greet people with a smile and a friendly greeting. Use "Hello" or "Good morning" when you enter a shop, a restaurant, or a public place. Courtesy and mutual respect are much appreciated in Irish culture.

Pubs and alcoholic beverages: Pubs are a central element of Irish culture, but it's important to consume alcohol responsibly. The legal age for drinking alcohol in Ireland is 18 years. Remember to drink responsibly and respect other pub guests. If you participate in a music session in a pub, listen attentively and don't interrupt the musicians during their performances.

Language and dialects: While English is the official language in Ireland, there is also a strong tradition of speaking the Gaelic (Irish) language. Although it's not necessary to speak Irish to visit the country, a simple "Thank you" (in Irish: "Go raibh maith agat") or "Hello" (in Irish: "Dia duit") can be appreciated by locals.

Time and punctuality: In Irish culture, importance is given to socializing and informal conversations. Therefore, people might be more relaxed about times and schedules. However, it's still good practice to be punctual for appointments and scheduled events.

Driving and road rules: If you rent a car and drive in Ireland, remember that driving is on the left. Familiarize yourself with Irish road rules and respect speed limits. Be courteous to other motorists and pedestrians.

Respect for sacred places: Ireland is home to numerous churches and sacred sites. When visiting these places, show respect and observe the instructions, like covering shoulders and legs if required. Avoid disturbing ongoing ceremonies or prayers.

Respect for the environment: Ireland is famous for its breathtaking landscapes and unspoiled nature. Contribute to preserving the environment by following local rules on waste collection and disposing of waste in the appropriate containers. Respect local fauna and flora, avoiding damaging or collecting protected plants or flowers.

Responsible fun: During your stay in Ireland, you might participate in parties or events. Remember to have fun responsibly and respect other participants. Avoid behavior that could disturb public order or cause discomfort to others.

By respecting these local norms and customs, you will immerse yourself in Irish culture, enjoy a warm welcome, and contribute to maintaining a pleasant environment for yourself and other visitors.

CHAPTER 7: Useful Information on Credit Cards and Currency

7.1 Accepted Credit Cards

During your trip to Ireland, you can rely on credit cards as a widely accepted method of payment. However, it is important to know some key information to avoid inconveniences and maximize the benefits of your credit cards.

The main credit cards accepted in Ireland include Visa, Mastercard, and American Express. These are generally accepted at hotels, restaurants, shops, and tourist attractions throughout the country. It is advisable to carry at least one of these cards to facilitate payments.

Before leaving for Ireland, make sure to contact your bank or your credit card issuer to inform them of your trip. This will prevent your transactions from being blocked for security reasons.

It is important to be aware of any international

fees associated with using credit cards in Ireland. Some cards may apply a small percentage as a fee for international transactions. Verify this information with your bank or card issuer before traveling.

Some smaller businesses, particularly in rural areas or villages, may only accept cash payments. Make sure you always have some cash on you, especially if you plan to visit more remote places. Also, we recommend always having some local currency for small expenses like public transportation or tips.

Lastly, always keep an eye on the safety of your credit cards during the trip. Avoid letting them out of sight, regularly check your balance, and keep emergency copies of contact numbers to report any losses or theft.

With this information on the credit cards accepted in Ireland and the precautions to take, you will be ready to handle your financial transactions safely and conveniently during your trip. Take advantage of the convenience and security offered by credit cards, allowing you to focus on the wonders that Ireland has to offer.

7.2 Cash Withdrawals

During your trip to Ireland, you may need to withdraw cash for some expenses or for situations where credit cards may not be accepted. Here are some helpful tips for withdrawing cash efficiently and safely.

ATMs: ATMs are widely available throughout Ireland, in both major cities and rural areas. Look for banks or ATM branches nearby to withdraw cash. Make sure to use reliable and safe ATMs, preferably those inside banks or in well-frequented places.

Fees: Some banks may charge a small fee for cash withdrawals made abroad. Contact your bank to know about the fees associated with withdrawing cash in Ireland and consider whether it is convenient to withdraw large amounts at once to reduce expenses. Also, try to avoid using private ATMs as they may charge higher fees.

Withdrawal Limits: Check if your bank has set daily or weekly limits for cash withdrawals.

Make sure you have a clear idea of the imposed limits to plan your cash withdrawals according to your needs.

Safety Measures: During cash withdrawals, always pay attention to your surroundings and ensure no one is watching as you enter your PIN or check your balance. Keep cash hidden in a safe place, such as a wallet with a zip closure or an inside pocket of your purse.

Alternatives: In addition to ATMs, you can also consider other options to get cash in Ireland. Some supermarkets, post offices, or currency exchange agencies may offer currency exchange services or allow cash withdrawals through card payments.

Remember to withdraw only the amount of cash you actually need to avoid carrying large amounts of money with you. In case of loss or theft of your debit or credit card, immediately contact your bank to report the incident and request a replacement card.

By following these tips, you will be able to withdraw cash safely and efficiently during your trip to Ireland, ensuring that you will always have access to the funds needed for your requirements.

7.3 Currency Exchange

During your trip to Ireland, you may need to exchange your currency to Euros, the official currency of the country. Here are some helpful tips for obtaining the best exchange rate and managing currency exchange conveniently.

Currency Exchange Offices: Look for reliable currency exchange offices, which offer competitive exchange rates and reduced fees. Airports, main railway stations, and tourist areas may have currency exchange offices available for your use.

Exchange Fees: Check if the exchange offices charge fees for the currency exchange service. Some offices might charge a small fee or a margin on the exchange rate, so compare different options to get the best possible deal.

Online Exchange Rates: Before leaving for Ireland, check the exchange rates online to have an idea of what the average exchange rate is. This will allow you to be more aware of the rates offered by exchange offices and to identify any excessively high or inconvenient fees.

Cash Exchange vs. Credit Cards: Consider whether it is more convenient to exchange a sum of cash or to use credit cards for payments. Credit cards usually offer a more favorable exchange rate compared to currency exchange services, but they might be subject to international fees. Carefully evaluate the options depending on your needs and personal preferences.

Security Tips: When exchanging currency, it is advisable to do so in a safe place and carefully check the money received. Keep the exchange receipts as proof for any future claims. Also, avoid displaying large amounts of money in public to minimize the risk of thefts or robberies.

By following these tips, you will be able to manage currency exchange conveniently and get the best possible exchange rate during your trip to Ireland. Take the time necessary to evaluate the available options and remember to exchange only at reliable places to ensure the security of your financial transactions.

7.4 Currency Management

During your trip to Ireland, it is important to manage your currency in a safe and convenient way. Here are some tips to help you best manage your money during your Irish experience.

Splitting Money: To avoid losing all your money in case of loss or theft, it is advisable to split it among several safe places. Keep a portion in a wallet or bag that you always carry with you, and leave another portion in a safe place, such as the hotel safe. This way, you will be protected in case an unforeseen event occurs.

Anti-Theft Wallets: Consider buying an anti-theft wallet that offers additional protections for your money and credit cards. These wallets come with zippers or snap closures that make it difficult for pickpockets to access the contents.

Emergency Copies of Credit Cards: Before

leaving, take a picture of your credit cards and keep them in a safe place as a backup. In case of loss or theft of the cards, you will have the necessary information to immediately report the situation to your bank and request a replacement card.

Insurance Coverage: Check if your travel insurance offers coverage for loss or theft of money. This could reimburse you for a portion or the full amount in case of accidents.

Use of Local Currency: Make sure you always have a bit of local currency with you for small expenses, such as public transportation or tips. Keep in mind that some small businesses might only accept cash.

Take care of your currency during your trip to Ireland by following these simple practices. With good financial management, you will be able to enjoy your trip worry-free and fully focus on the beauties of Ireland.

7.5 Useful Information on Credit Cards and Money

During your trip to Ireland, it is essential to be well-informed about how to manage your credit cards and money safely and efficiently. Here are some useful tips to help you best handle your finances during your Irish adventure.

While traveling in Ireland, most shops, hotels, and restaurants accept major credit cards like Visa, Mastercard, and American Express. However, it is always advisable to carry more than one credit card to ensure a backup option in case of problems with one of the cards.

ATMs are widely available throughout Ireland, allowing you to withdraw cash conveniently. However, keep in mind that there may be fees for international withdrawals. Check with your bank or card issuer for any fees associated with foreign withdrawals.

If you need to exchange your currency for euros, you can do so at currency exchange offices or banks in Ireland. It's advisable to compare exchange rates offered by different institutions to get the best deal. Avoid exchanging currency at airports, as they usually offer less favorable exchange rates.

During your trip, ensure the safety of your credit cards. Avoid leaving cards unattended or out of sight, regularly check your balance, and keep emergency copies of contact numbers to report any loss or theft.

Be vigilant and aware of possible scams or financial fraud during your trip. Avoid providing personal or financial information to unknown individuals or websites. Use secure internet connections and closely monitor your financial transactions to detect any suspicious activity.

By following these useful tips, you can manage your credit cards and money effectively during your trip to Ireland. Enjoy your experience with peace of mind, knowing that you have taken the necessary precautions to ensure financial security.

Conclusion

It's time to conclude this extraordinary journey through Ireland, guided by our

"Ireland in the Heart: Pocket Travel Guide 2023." We hope you have found this comprehensive and engaging guide an indispensable companion in your exploration of the Emerald Isle. We trust it has provided you with an unforgettable and meaningful experience, allowing you to discover the hidden wonders of this captivating island.

We began our journey by exploring the geography and climate of Ireland, immersing ourselves in the diverse and captivating landscape, from the rugged coastline to the lush green hills. We delved into the country's history, traversing the ages from ancient Celtic civilizations to independence, uncovering how this land has shaped its unique identity and culture.

The top destinations took us on a discovery of Irish gems, from vibrant Dublin to the grandeur of the Cliffs of Moher. We embraced Irish culture, dancing to the tune of folk music, uncovering the secrets of leprechaun legends, and savoring traditional dishes like the famous Irish Stew and irresistible oysters.

We explored historical museums and castles, such as the National Museum of Ireland and the enchanting Kylemore Castle, giving us a window into the past and a deeper understanding of this fascinating land's history.

The guide provided practical information, tips, and itineraries to help you craft a tailor-made journey tailored to your interests and passions. We offered advice on the best time to visit Ireland, how to get around, and what to pack, ensuring you are well-prepared for your trip.

We delved into managing your credit cards and money wisely during your journey, ensuring greater financial peace of mind. In addition to providing practical information, we also delved into Irish culture, from the Gaelic language to art, literature, and dance, helping you fully immerse yourself in the richness of this captivating culture.

Lastly, we offered itineraries ranging from a few days to a ten-day adventure, allowing you to discover the diverse facets and hidden treasures of this magical land.

We conclude this guide with an invitation: immerse yourself in the heart of Ireland, with the spirit of a curious explorer and an open heart. Let yourself be enveloped by the beauty of the landscape, the fascinating legends, and the warm hospitality of its people. Explore the culture and history of this unique land, uncover its hidden secrets, and be inspired by its authenticity.

Always remember that Ireland is much more than a tourist destination. It is a place that touches the heart and soul, captivating you with its beauty and embracing you with the warmth of its people. Whether you are planning your first visit or returning to immerse yourself once more in its magic, know that Ireland will always welcome you with open arms.

Thank you for choosing "Ireland in the Heart: Pocket Travel Guide 2023." We are honored to have accompanied you on this journey, and we hope to have provided you with a unique and unforgettable experience. May your journey through Ireland be filled with emotions, discoveries, and special moments, leaving you with memories to last a lifetime. Safe travels!

HERE IS YOU FREE GIFT!

10 RECOMMENDED ITINERARIES

FOR YOUR TRIP TO IRELAND.

SCAN HERE TO DOWNLOAD IT

Made in the USA
Coppell, TX
02 March 2024